The Soul of My Son:

A Grieving Father's Journey

from Skeptic to Psychic Medium

by Steven Joseph

Printed in the United States of America

First Printing, 2016

ISBN 978-0-692-77473-1

Steven Joseph
Intuitive Visionary Concepts LLC d/b/a The Tall Medium
P.O. Box 45368
Omaha, NE 68145
www.tallmedium.com

Cover layout by Audrey Burn Graphic Design
www.audreyburn.com

Preface

I am the last person I ever imagined would write a book. Mostly because I have always been a guarded person who only shared my thoughts with a select few. However, things have since changed. As I have found out during this lifetime, things can change in an instant. This is the story of my unique and unusual journey through these dramatic changes.

I was the ultimate skeptic of spirit communication and anything that couldn't be explained by hard evidence. My life revolved around a wife, two children, reasonably nice possessions and a somewhat enjoyable career. All of that was turned upside down on one fateful day. My youngest son Drew tragically took his own life at the age of twenty, setting into motion a series of events that led to my spiritual awakening. During the course of less than three years, I evolved from ultimate skeptic to psychic medium and spiritual mentor. While taking a shower one morning, my son visited me in spirit and implanted the idea of writing this book. He even gave me the title. Since then my wife, friends and some clients urged me to tell my story as they found it to be interesting. My hope is that you do as well.

I have written numerous blog articles about spirituality and its relation to the grief process, but never an undertaking like this book. My belief is that all creativity is divinely inspired by spirit. Just as in my psychic medium readings, I am a channel from spirit, guided to put forth a message. If this book helps others recognize their spirituality or move through their grief process, it was well worth my time and effort.

The cover photo is of Drew and myself, standing on a small island outcropping, barely big enough for the two of us. It was taken during the summer of 2007 at Catamount Reservoir, near Pikes Peak Highway in Colorado. That little pebble covered island had emerged due to low water levels at the reservoir. We had traveled to one of his track meets in Colorado Springs and had time afterward for some family activities.

Dedication

I would like to thank a few people for their belief in me and persistence in urging me to put pen to paper. My wife Karen, who brought our sons into this world and shared with us a special bond that has kept our family so close-knit. She has always been highly spiritual and believes in me every step of the way as I discover more about my spiritual gifts. My oldest son Eric, who is not quite ready to awaken and embrace his spirituality but still understands why I am who I am.

My fellow colleague Kevin, who was the first psychic medium we visited after Drew's passing. After learning of the signs I was receiving from spirit, he invited us to a psychic development group. It was in that group where I gave my first medium reading, which set this entire process into motion. Another medium and colleague, Angie, who is one of the most positive and upbeat people I have ever known. She has encouraged my development from the first time we met and has continued to help me along the way. It was with her that I did my first gallery reading and learned so much about my potential.

My friend, fellow medium and spiritual mirror, Jen. It was her prodding me with spirit messages from my son that finally got me to begin writing this book. She was also given a concept for the cover of this book by Drew, which was masterfully designed by my friend Audrey.

Last but not least, my sister Debbie. She has been very accepting of, and interested in my spiritual journey. Her thoughtful input and grammatical review of my first draft proved useful in helping me expand in some areas, while polishing a few others. Her strong background in education, combined with being a spiritual "outsider" was invaluable in refining my message for those who would benefit from it the most.

The Skeptic

I was the ultimate skeptic. In my mind, psychics, mediums, tarot cards, energy healers, ghost hunters and the like were all scams and con artists. I wholeheartedly believed they were all preying on gullible people to make a buck. They were of no use to me, other than to make fun of on occasion. On the other hand, my wife Karen has always had a curious interest in all things spiritual and metaphysical. Whether it was the cable TV show about the sisters with supernatural abilities, the weekly network series about a woman who was visited by ghosts or reality shows about psychic mediums, she watched them all. I never understood why she was so interested in these shows, so we just agreed to disagree. On occasion, she would be watching a particular show about a famous medium from the east coast as I walked through the living room. My response would be shaking my head and asking her why she watched that crap. As is normal for most married couples, there are certain subjects one partner just isn't going to change the other partner's mind about. The supernatural and metaphysical was one of those subjects for us.

My daily life didn't involve any consideration of the supposed spirit world. One reason was that I had been raised in the Roman Catholic Church. Religion didn't resonate with me because it was not provable and frankly, didn't make sense to me. It was all too grandiose, contrived and unbelievable for my pragmatic life view. Since I was a child and had no say in my own religious choice, I went along with the charade until the age of eighteen. As an adult, nobody could force me to go to church and embrace their beliefs. It was then that I left the church and now consider myself a "recovering Catholic." That resistance may have carried over into spiritual beliefs. I didn't know that religion and spirituality were two completely different things at the time but it didn't matter. Neither religion nor spirituality were going to play a role in my life or influence my decisions. One point Karen and I always agreed on was letting our boys find their own way to whatever faith or beliefs they chose. They both expressed occasional curiosity but never enough to join a church or pursue a religion.

I went about my existence without religious or spiritual beliefs. I lived a life that would be considered moral by any religious standards. Yes, I made mistakes like everyone else but I didn't feel compelled to tell a stranger about them in a tiny room at a church. The concept of a God creating the universe in seven days was a scientifically disproven myth to me. I considered heaven, hell and purgatory as myths, conjured up by man to keep people tied to religion through fear. As it turns out, I was right about those beliefs. The thought of our souls, or spirits, existing beyond the physical lifetime was simply not practical or believable to me. People claiming to communicate with those spirits were ridiculous and downright laughable. As it turns out, I was judging people in a similar fashion to how I didn't want to be judged. For most of my life, I didn't care about spirituality. I was set in my beliefs and there was no convincing me otherwise. Unless you had black-and-white proof to present, I was immovable on the subject of religion and spirituality. For 52 years anyway.

My Son Drew

Drew was planned nearly to the day, just like his older brother Eric. We wanted Eric to be walking around and out of diapers before another baby came along. With a 20 month gap between the two, that plan worked out very well. Drew was born at the end of November after a much shorter labor than his brother. He was a little larger at 9 lbs 14 ounces and 22-1/2" long. His size was not all that surprising, given the fact that his parents are both taller than average. The surprise for me was when he came out with a full head of bright red hair. It wasn't a surprise for Karen. She had dreams throughout her pregnancy that we were going to have a red-headed child. I dismissed those as ridiculous because I was skeptical of anything extra-sensory or supernatural. Dreams and premonitions were nothing but ridiculous and nonsensical to me. Little did I know that bright red hair would be a sign of his bright and fiery personality. A rare combination of red hair and blue eyes was just another indication of how unique and special he was. I now had two boys I could love and cherish, watch them discover the world and help achieve their hopes and dreams.

My world somehow seemed complete and the best times were ahead of me.

Drew was a big boy, to say the least. He had what Karen called "linebacker thighs" and was in the top one percent of the physical growth charts throughout his childhood. In addition to being big and strong for his age, he was also very smart, with a compassionate soul and a magnetic personality. Eric welcomed his younger brother and they spent countless hours playing together, despite their age difference. We have a cherished photo of Eric sitting on the sofa and giving his newborn baby brother a kiss on the forehead. They grew to become polar opposites in their hobbies and pastimes by middle school but always had their unspoken brotherly bond. Drew developed into a very athletic child and friendly competition became a driving force for him. I recall an instance from early in elementary school. I believe he was in first grade and they had an end-of-year class picnic at the park. That evening he informed us that he had won every competition at the picnic. Running race, shoe kick and other similar events. I was a little skeptical of his claim and said; "You couldn't have won EVERY event." Drew wasn't one to brag about accomplishments and the most important part of the day was having fun with his friends. A few days later, I was talking with a parent who had been a volunteer at the class picnic. I told him about Drew's wild claim of winning every event. The dad then informed me that yes, Drew had in fact, won EVERY event.

He started playing soccer at the age of five and was a big contributor to a very successful team over the next five years. I still have fond memories of him running down the field, kicking the ball and seeing boys from the opposing team try to knock him off the ball. They were never successful and usually ended up bouncing off of Drew's much larger frame. However, many of those soccer teammates gravitated to him and even looked up to him like a big brother and protector. Baseball overlapped for three years and after being an assistant coach for Eric's team, I coached Drew's team for all three of those seasons. His drive and determination, along with participating in practices with the older boys on Eric's team had made him a good baseball player too. Those older boys took a liking to Drew and many even hung around after practice to field balls when Drew got his turn to step up to the plate and take a few swings. Other kids just liked being around him. I guess most would call it a magnetic personality but I feel they could sense his kind and fun-loving soul. One could just tell from being around him that he was accepting, with unconditional love and a zest for life.

Baseball wasn't his passion and he found the lack of continuous action too boring. My parents had given him a plastic street hockey stick and ball as a gift when he was about seven years old. He would stand in the driveway and hit that ball against the garage door and we didn't think much of it. Then one day he came inside and announced; "I want to play hockey." My response was "Isn't that what you are doing?" He immediately and insistently replied "No, I want to play on ice!" Not knowing how committed he would be to this venture, we scrambled to a used sporting goods store and found him a pair of ice skates. It turned out to be the perfect time of year to enroll him in the initiation program of our local ice hockey league. He was a natural on the ice and once he finally learned the "hockey stop" there was no holding him back. We had always encouraged our boys to pursue activities they had a passion for and this was his new passion. After completing the initiation program, he tried out for a travel team to see how he compared in ability with others his age. He made the Mite B team and it didn't take long to find his niche as a talented defenseman. I could see the excitement he felt from this newfound avenue of adventure and I was excited for him.

We traveled to all of the out of town games and tournaments, with Eric accompanying us. Karen's job required her to work most Saturdays, so it was usually the boys and I bonding for a weekend. We made countless wonderful memories during those weekend trips. The first three seasons we were a trio, before Eric was old enough to stay home by himself. Eric enthusiastically operated the scoreboard at almost every rink we went to. Despite Eric not being a hockey player, he and Drew always had something to talk about after the games. We enjoyed many games, hotel stays, meals and even tourist activities together. The two would watch movies in the back of the van while I listened to the movie and their silly comments.

It was during his third season of hockey that he was nicknamed "Cheeto." The team was in the dressing room changing before practice. As was usual for Drew, he was wearing orange shoes, long orange socks, orange athletic shorts and an orange shirt. He had long hair at the time, which was also "orange." One of his teammates remarked that he looked like a giant Cheeto. That nickname was embraced by his teammates, quickly adopted by the coaches and it stuck with him from that day forward.

While playing on the Bantam AA team during his sixth season of travel hockey, he began losing his love of the sport. While he liked the competition, an overbearing and verbally abusive coach took all the fun out of the game for Drew. Because of Drew's size and strength, his head coach wanted him to go out and pick fights with the more skilled players. We had raised a fine young man with a compassionate soul and this was not something he wanted to do. That decision affected his ice time for a while but the assistant coach got him moved to starting defenseman, which showcased his true value to the team. My 14 year old son had made a life decision based on his beliefs of right and wrong. He stood up for what he believed, I supported him and that is still one of the things about him that makes me the most proud.

That final season of hockey also happened to be when his physical education teacher and track coach discovered him as an athlete with incredible ability. One of the physical assessments was the shuttle run. It is a back-and-forth, stop-and-go test of agility and quickness. Drew had come within less than a second of the school record. A pretty impressive feat, given his size. The record for that event was held by a former student who happened to be a major college football player and Heisman Trophy winner. Drew quickly learned discus and shot put, winning both events in almost every middle school meet for two seasons.

Perhaps more importantly, he was like an assistant coach, helping the other throwers improve their techniques. Sometimes he even stayed late after practice to help another athlete. That is who Drew was. He was willing to help if you were willing to learn. He broke school and district meet records in shot put, discus and the 4 X 400 relay. During his freshman season in high school, he competed at the varsity level and lettered all four years. His interest in those events tapered off when he discovered the hammer throw, which quickly became his new passion. Drew dedicated himself to training more than he had in any other event and broke the state records for both young men's age groups. The two of us traveled to track meets as far away as Colorado, Minnesota, Illinois and Tennessee. After his junior year, he was offered an athletic scholarship and signed a letter of intent with the University of Missouri. That school also had a good business program, which was his planned major. He had a dream and I was extremely pleased to see him pursue it with such vigor.

Despite his success as an athlete and a good student, Drew had plenty of ups and downs. His athletic performance and attentiveness in class sometimes had wide swings. Most notable was his extreme inconsistency in the throwing events. While consistently using the same technique, there were great variances in his distances from day to day. We also began seeing sudden bursts of anger that were atypical of his personality. After numerous tests, Drew was diagnosed with thyroiditis. It was not hyperthyroidism or hypothyroidism but a condition causing extreme swings back and forth between the two. This diagnosis explained what was happening with our son.

Both of our boys were always very smart and able to get good grades without bringing home much homework. They both participated in the elementary school High Ability Learning Program and in high school, both were accepted into the International Baccalaureate program. High school credits were never a problem until the end of Drew's senior year. He had one book report to finish for his English class while also practicing for and competing in the district and state track meets. His teacher had given him extra time, due to his athletic commitments but something happened to change that. We still don't know if it was his teachers disdain for athletes or a decision by the principal but suddenly he was informed that late work was not allowed. It became a battle pitting Drew, myself, Karen and his school counselor against the principal. Drew lost that battle and could not graduate with his class. He made up the class in summer school and received his diploma but his Division I collegiate eligibility was gone. Because of eligibility requirements, his scholarship was also gone. His hopes and dreams were destroyed. There was an option to compete at the Division II level for a season and several schools were interested but the timing required him to sit out a year. He was never the same. His focus shifted from college to just doing what he wanted to do. His interests change and his circle of friends became smaller. We will never know whether the change was due to the thyroid condition, his dream of competing as a Division I athlete vanishing, or both.

After high school, he worked and saved money to buy his own vehicle. It was a 1997 Ford F-350 dually with a 7.3 litre Powerstroke diesel engine. I had to include the exact details because he would have wanted me to. This truck quickly became one of his new interests. As was the case in everything he did, Drew quickly learned all about diesel engines. He spent a lot of his spare time working on that truck, fixing, upgrading, accessorizing and customizing. He was a unique individual and wanted his vehicle to be unique too. After cutting holes in his truck bed to install 5" diameter exhaust stacks, some of his friends gave him a second nick name, "Stacks." He loved driving and working on trucks, the bigger the better. He loved working with his hands. His employer gave him a few opportunities to drive a tractor-trailer truck. After seeing him drive my pickup while pulling a trailer, I knew he would naturally be good at it, and he was.

About six months before Drew passed, a business partner visited me from Israel. Avishay is a few years older than me and brought along his youngest son Nadav, who is about Drew's age. The four of us spent the day together, touring our city and visiting an aerospace museum. After we left the museum, the four of us sat down for dinner and ended up talking for hours. Our conversation started with sharing information about our families and lifestyle but quickly turned to current socioeconomic and political issues. Drew had more input than any of us, surprising both myself and Avishay with his vast awareness and knowledge of these issues. This boy I raised had become a well-educated, level-headed, tolerant and compassionate young man. At one point in the conversation, my business partner told Drew that he should become a politician, because he had some very good solutions to the world's problems. I couldn't have been more proud of him.

A couple months before his passing he began removing some of the accessories from his motorcycle so he could sell it. He wanted to attend truck driving school because it was a prerequisite to becoming a diesel mechanic. I gave him our credit card to pay the $4,000.00 for truck driving school. He quit his job to make time for the four week course. He had completed one of the four weeks and told us about the high praise he received from his instructors. As in so many other things in his life, Drew was held out as an example for the other students because of his ability to learn quickly. There would be no second week of school but we have the video of his driving portion each day, taken from various angles inside and outside the truck.

Drew had girlfriends almost all of his time throughout high school. His first girlfriend unknowingly taught him a life lesson in right and wrong. She was somewhat of an instigator and often tried to get him to fight other guys. At 6 feet 4 inches, 250 lbs, with his weight training, he could have taken on just about anyone and come out on top. That wasn't who he was. Drew was always the peacemaker. He was the anti-bully. When someone would bully a small kid or a minority, Drew would befriend the underdog and hang out with them. He didn't actively intimidate anyone but they knew any bullying of his friends would have to go through him. Nobody was ever up to that challenge. Kes was his last girlfriend. We didn't know about her and didn't get to meet her while Drew was still physically alive. We only got to see them together in photos she shared with us after his passing. Drew was 20 years old and she was not quite 17 years old. He felt we would question the relationship because of the age difference and chose not to bring it out into the open. As it turns out she is a wonderful young woman who we would have been honored to call our daughter-in-law.

The Longest Day

Things were going pretty well for Karen and I. The boys were grown and independent, so we began pursuing some of our dreams. One of those dreams was finding a remote piece of land or even a small cabin in the mountains. Our plan was to live there from late spring through early fall when we retire and spend the winters down south in a recreational vehicle. We were taking advantage of a long weekend to drive southwest of Denver to look at potential properties. Before we left, I went downstairs to see Drew. It was Halloween night but he was at home and immersed in a car racing video game. He didn't say much, but when he was playing a video game he didn't like to be distracted. He gave no indication of being troubled or upset. Karen and I drove six of the nine hours and stopped at a motel just inside the Colorado border. It was just a pit stop, so we quickly moved our bags inside and went to sleep.

I woke up at about 5:30 in the morning and couldn't get back to sleep. Just after I showered and got dressed, my cell phone rang. It was a 911 dispatcher from back home. They had received a call from Drew's girlfriend and she feared he was going to attempt suicide. There were deputies at our house trying to get someone to answer the door. I woke Karen and had her call Eric. She told him to go downstairs and check on Drew. A couple minutes later he told her Drew was asleep. She told Eric to "wake him up!" His reply was "He has blood on his head." Our hearts dropped as Karen told him to let the deputies in.

Since I was immediately in shock, my conversation with the deputies is still somewhat of a blur. We were informed that Drew had a gunshot wound to the head. Paramedics were on scene and found some weak vital signs. They were transporting him via ambulance to the nearest trauma center. Eric was taken upstairs where deputies questioned him about what had happened. We quickly packed our bags and threw everything in my truck. This would be the longest drive of my life. I called my brother who lived a few miles from our house. He was a law enforcement officer and would be able to get accurate and updated information for us. He went to our house first and then to the hospital. I pressed him for details about Drew's condition but he would just say they are still working on him. I drove for about 20 minutes and began feeling faint, so I pulled over and let Karen drive. Within a couple minutes I had passed out in the passenger seat. I know now I was in a lucid state at that time but do not recall what I was shown or told. After calling my brother a couple more times and getting no particulars, I somehow knew Drew was not going to make it. It was a combination of what my brother was "not" saying, and unknown intuition, or "gut feeling" and most likely something I was shown during my unconscious episode. Imagine spending six hours in silence, with thoughts of every conceivable outcome running through your mind. I knew I could accept any condition he was left in, as long as he was still alive. Every time I analyzed all the possibilities, I kept arriving at the conclusion that my youngest son was now dead.

Upon our arrival at the hospital, we were quickly taken to a conference room along with Eric. An emergency room physician joined us to inform us of Drew's condition. He was brought in with a devastating head injury. Due to the extent of his injury, his brain had lost function and he was being kept on life support. That word, "devastating" still brings to mind that meeting every time I hear it. It seemed my life changed forever when I heard that word. All three of us cried and hugged each other while sitting in those chairs. There wasn't much more for the physician to say, so she left us in that room to absorb what she had told us and compose ourselves. I was suddenly numb emotionally. I didn't feel it at the time but someone later told me I was like a zombie. Internally, I was overwhelmed by the emotions of loss.

We went to Drew's room and the emotions hit us all over again. Our beautiful, amazing son was lying there with tubes attached to him. His loving and caring personality, intelligence, sense of humor, and incredible physical body were all gone in an instant. All of his hopes and dreams, all of our hopes and dreams for him would never come to pass. The burning question we were left with, why he had to do this, could never be answered.

Karen wanted desperately to hold his hand but they were covered with paper bags. We began the process of trying to hurry the investigators to take swabs from his hands for gunshot residue. Almost all of our family members were at the hospital but I felt the overpowering need for my sister to be here. She lived in California. I gave the information to my airline rewards account to my sister-in-law and let her make the arrangements.

We were asked to a meet with someone from the local organ donation organization. Drew had not signed up as an organ donor when he renewed his driver's license, so the decision would be ours. I already knew my answer was yes but Karen and I began discussing the options. After some discussion, we agreed that organ donation would help a lot of people, especially children. Drew loved children and found ways to interact and help them whenever he could. During the meeting, Karen specifically asked if we could direct Drew's organs to help children. Because of the waiting list system and his physical size, that was not possible. We gave permission and signed papers to donate his organs, tissue, etc. They would be able to use everything but his eyes. Due to the traumatic force of his injury, his eyes would not be usable for transplant. Now all that was left to do was wait for organ recipients to be lined up. The biggest problem was his lungs. At 6'4" tall and 240 lbs, Drew was a very large man. His chest and therefore his lungs, were very large. The medical staff came in his room several times to measure and re-measure his chest. We were informed they were having a hard time finding a recipient with a large enough chest cavity for Drew's lungs to fit into.

Karen initially wanted an open casket funeral. My grandparents had owned a mortuary and I grew up a few blocks away. Having spent time in and around the funeral home, I knew more details than most about that process. He would not look the same and I wanted to remember him as he was, without the mental picture of his face after an autopsy and embalming. I also did not want him buried at a cemetery because I would rather have his cremated remains with us at the house. My brother's wife took the responsibility of contacting funeral homes about arrangements. She presented options and had also found a church for a memorial service. We gave her the go ahead to make arrangements and are very appreciative of her willingness to take this responsibility off our hands during our most trying time.

After the whirlwind of activity calmed down, we spent some alone time with Drew. Very few people know the thoughts that run through your mind when losing a child. All the plans he may have had, potential wedding and watching him raise our grandchildren, finding a career he loved. Those thoughts and a million more filled our minds as we dwelled on what might have been but would never be. I felt emotional pain that physically hurt my heart. I experienced emptiness like you cannot imagine, that literally took my breath away. I was not a religious person but if there was a hell, I couldn't imagine it being worse than this.

The one question that kept coming to mind was, "why?" That question has the most complicated answer. The pragmatic and analytical answer is depression and escape from emotional pain. We had seen no indication beforehand and my immediate thoughts drew me back to the thyroid problems he had at about 15 years of age. That medical condition had caused some changes in him but nothing lasting. We conversed with Drew's girlfriend at the hospital and she informed us of some suicidal comments he had mad to her and her family. We were never made aware of those comments and they had been dismissed as offhand remarks. None of this internal speculation answered the lingering question of why he had done this.

Waiting Room Vision

The hospital had a small hotel wing for people in our situation and we got a room with two beds for Eric, Karen and myself. I checked us in and got Eric settled while Karen stayed with Drew. I laid on the bed for a few minutes but could not sleep. Eric fell asleep and I just watched him. My fatherly protective instinct went into overdrive. I was now scared to leave Eric alone. Of course my fears were unfounded but when you suddenly go from two sons to one, everything changes. That room was the equivalent of about a city block from where Drew was. I walked it many, many times, checking in on both of my sons. From Drew's room, through the secure door, down the elevator, around the corner, down the hall, hallway jogs to the left, through the double doors, another hall, to the left, down a flight of stairs, around the balcony to Eric's room. I call it Eric's room because I never slept there. I tried to sleep a couple times but gave up.

On the second night, after one of my round trips to see Eric and back, I decided to sit in the waiting room. It was early in the morning, maybe two or three o'clock. I still had not slept, showered or shaved. The TV on the wall was on, I think it was a cable sports network. I stared at the TV but didn't know or care what was on. Then I leaned my head back and closed my eyes for a few seconds. Just as I was on the verge of dozing off to sleep, there he was, clear as day. Drew. With his big cheesy smile and slight red beard. I was startled. This could not be real. Things like that didn't happen to me. I was the ultimate skeptic of clairvoyance and all things metaphysical or supernatural. My heart was racing and I didn't know why. I wasn't scared but the unexpected nature of this vision had startled me. I didn't tell anyone about this vision but I will never forget it. In retrospect, I know this was a clairvoyant vision because I was not asleep, or in a lucid, pre-sleep state. Why then and there? My defenses were down. My pragmatic personality and denial of this type of thing were not even in my thought process. Basically, I was "open" to his visit at that moment.

That same night as I was walking the halls I kept hearing the lyrics "Oh, I just gotta know. If you're really there, and you really care" from a Def Leppard song entitled "Foolin." I had no idea at the time why this song was continually running through my head. Spirit communication through music was not on my radar nor in my realm of belief or understanding.

Letting Go

By the third day, all the organ recipients were in place and it was time for Drew to give of himself in one final, heroic act. At one point, there had been an apparent miscalculation by the hospital staff resulting in an uncomfortable situation. We were all in the waiting room and Karen was with her sister near the check in counter. A man approached the counter and informed the staff he was there for his heart transplant. For Karen, hearing those words was like a sledgehammer to the chest. We knew it was inevitable but this wasn't something we needed to hear. Karen's sister informed our nursing staff and our family and friends were moved to another waiting area inside the patient room area. I hadn't heard the words but had seen the man approach the counter. He was older than me, maybe in his late fifties. I hope his gift has helped to improve his quality of life and extend the time he can spend with his family.

The transplant team and procedure was in place and had probably been done a thousand times by this hospital staff but for us, it was our last goodbye. This was a defining moment in our lives and all the medical professionals knew it. We were assured there would be a moment of silence and prayer by the medical staff prior to beginning the operations and ending his physical life. The utmost care and respect of all those involved will never be forgotten. Karen and I had a few minutes alone with Drew and then they placed him on a gurney. We accompanied him to the elevator with my brother and Karen's sister. It was there we said our last goodbyes. The image of that moment is forever etched in my memory.

Saying Goodbye

The memorial service was delayed until the following Saturday, mostly to accommodate the back surgery my brother had scheduled. That delay gave us plenty of time to find and order an urn for his ashes. We found one that was an unusual orange pattern with black accent. To us, it almost looked like a pile of Cheetos. In addition to his name, birth and passing dates, Karen chose a saying to fill the last available lines: "Always loved, never forgotten." We had also ordered silver necklaces with Drew's photo etched on the front. His name, birth and passing dates were etched on the back. Each necklace held a small amount of his ashes and a strand of hair from his scruffy beard. We still wear those necklaces every day.

Karen and I each wore one of Drew's shirts. I wore his pink dress shirt and pink tennis shoes, with my own gray dress slacks. I felt that is what he would have wanted and it just felt right to me. In keeping with typical "Drew" style of unique, non-conformist and often trend-setting, I didn't care what anyone thought. This was my son and my statement. It was my way of honoring his true personality, that I had often lovingly poked fun at. I drove his truck to the church, hung a colorful floral wreath I had purchased on the tailgate and parked where everyone in attendance would have to walk by it. My sister, Karen's sister and some family friends had come to our house and gathered many reminders of Drew from his possessions. Photos, countless athletic medals, jerseys, and even a hockey stick were laid out on two tables for people to view and reminisce. We picked some music that was meaningful to us and some from the playlist on Drew's phone. The minister performed a brief ceremony and read something I had written about Drew, his accomplishments and who he was. My brother's wife and in-laws arranged for barbecue and side dishes to be served after the service by one of Drew's favorite chain restaurants.

Relatives, friends, former coaches and teammates all showed up to remember Drew. Some people who reminded us later that they had talked with us at the service, we had not realized were there. We didn't realize it at the time but Karen and I were still in a fog. Neither of us remember many of the people who were there until we reviewed the guest book months later. It was amazing to see how well loved he was, the amount of people who experienced his special brand of love in so few years.

Ringing Ears, etc.

About three weeks after Drew's passing. I began waking up in the morning with song lyrics playing in my head. The lyrics were meaningful, with some relation to current or past experiences with Drew. I had no idea why or how but somehow I believed those song lyrics may have been sent from beyond by Drew. I started keeping a list of the songs on my computer and soon began adding signs and dreams. I had no idea why but felt compelled to document it all. Maybe it was to convince my skeptical self or maybe it was because I was meant to eventually write this book and would need the documentation.

I had stopped listening to music when Drew passed because it seemed every song I heard brought up sad memories. I subscribed to a satellite radio package of only news and talk, to avoid hearing any music. But somehow these songs brought meaning to me and I needed to listen to them. So I started keeping a list of songs, reading the lyrics, downloading them to my phone and listening to them. As I look back, the song list tells a story of my grief process. Starting with lyrics about loss and pain, the first one I received were "There's a Hole in My Heart That Can Only Be Filled by You." One of the most notable and memorable was a song entitled "I Drive Your Truck." I am partial to rock & roll and have never been a fan of country music but this song was on Drew's playlist and he even had the CD in his truck. We had listened to some of his music while driving to Pittsburgh a few months earlier. I didn't pay attention to the lyrics of "I Drive Your Truck" and somehow thought it was about a son losing his father. The song is actually about a father losing his son. I proceeded to burn this song onto a CD and played it every time I drove Drew's truck. It brought tears to my eyes every time for several months. It is said that tears of sorrow are healing and I truly believe that to be true. Listening to the music he had sent me had unleashed powerful emotions, while helping to open my heart, mind and soul.

That song about driving the truck is just one example of a music library that has grown to over 200 songs. All of them received out of nowhere, usually between one and three lines of each song. Some were songs I had never heard before and had to research to find them based on a few lyrics or a melody. Just one more piece of evidence pointing to my awakening was the fact that I received lyrics to a song I had never heard before. On many days, the lyrics were to songs I had previously received. That was due to a message I needed to continue receiving until I understood.

About a week later, Karen and I began experiencing unexplainable, temporary quirks and malfunctions of electronics. Cell phones, the stove, furnace and lights were doing strange things. Then one evening I was carrying laundry down to the laundry room. Out of the corner of my eye, I saw a tiny, bright orange light near the ceiling in the dark basement. The basement had been Drew's "man cave" and bedroom. The blinds were closed, all the lights were off and I could find no explanation for where the light had come from. Orange had always been Drew's favorite color, so I took it as another sign from him.

Later that day, December 11th, I began experiencing continuous high pitched tones, or "ringing" in my ears. So I opened up a popular internet search engine and began searching. Most of what I came across at first was a medical condition known as tinnitus. There was apparently no known cause or known cure. Then I stumbled upon a website that listed ringing ears as a symptom of spiritual awakening. Since the medical community had no answers, it was worth a look. Suddenly it made sense. Several websites listed symptoms of spiritual awakening. I was experiencing many of them. Some of these symptoms could be attributed to the shock of Drew's passing but not all of them. A few examples of these were:

Amplification of the senses

Vivid dreams

Creativity bursts

Synchronous numbers i.e. 11:11, 4:44, etc.

Yearning for deeper meaning

Increased integrity

Searching for purpose

Hold on a minute here! This information was way outside my comfort zone. What I found was leading me into the supernatural realm. I was not ready for this. Being the pragmatic type, I needed more convincing evidence and concrete proof. After all, I was the guy who playfully mocked my wife for watching TV shows about mediums and supernatural abilities. I would have to swallow my pride and rebuild my entire belief system to embrace these new findings.

Those signs continued the following Sunday morning and became more frequent. I was awakened by the beeping of my travel alarm clock. This alarm clock had not been used since our last trip, the morning Drew took his own life. As I turned off the alarm clock, it read 4:44. This alarm clock had always been set to 6:00 a.m. About a minute later I heard the floor creak in the hallway outside the bedroom, just as if someone had stepped on the one spot that made noise. Karen and Eric were both asleep in bed. I believed it was Drew sending me a message. A couple hours later, I woke up and walked out to the living room. Some of my research had led me to meditation as a means to connecting with spirits of loved ones who had passed. I still missed Drew terribly and was willing to try anything. Sitting on the sofa, I lit a candle and tried to meditate. I fell asleep and was awakened from a dream. In this dream, I was sitting in my usual spot on the sofa and watched Karen walk over to the window and peek out the blinds. Drew walked out from down the hall behind me, turned down the stairs and said something indiscernible. I turned to watch him walk down the stairs and asked him "What, what, what did you say?" After no response from Drew, I got up and walked down the stairs but did not find him. His bed was still there with gray bedding. (In reality it had pink sheets but had been taken by the cleanup crew) I walked over and fell face down onto his bed, at which point I was abruptly awakened. At that time, I knew nothing of dream interpretation and wasn't sure what to think. Most important to me was that I saw my son. Whether it was real or not didn't matter. It felt real to me and left me with a feeling of comfort.

Soon after that, I was lying on my back in bed one night, trying to sleep. Just as I began to doze off, I heard knocking on the bedroom window. Strange. This window was at least twelve feet off the ground. I heard a couple more knocks, then I saw a vision of Drew's face. He had on his favorite dark sunglasses and was holding a hammer in an upright position, as if he were hammering a nail. He then turned his head a little to the left, acknowledging that I had seen him and gave me a big smile. This was a similar situation to the vision I had in the hospital waiting room but I was not startled this time. I stayed relaxed, welcomed him and it was an amazing feeling. Despite the vision only lasting a few seconds, I was immediately relaxed and easily fell asleep.

A few days later I was at the gas station fueling my truck. Everything I had experienced since his passing was leading me toward releasing the need for his physical presence and seeking his spiritual connection. I was talking out loud to Drew, telling him I love him, miss him and forgive him and hope he was guided to the light to find his peace. I told him I wished he would send me a sign that he found the light. I stared across the street at the sky above a little pond in front of a new hotel as I waited for the gas pump to finish. Just to the left of where I was looking, a big green "H" flickered and lit up on the Holiday Inn Express hotel sign. Nothing else, just the "H" which I took as my sign that he had found "the light." It was reassuring and comforted me to know that not only had he found the light but that he could also somehow let me know.

I could write an entire book about just the signs we have received from Drew. The tangible signs include pennies, feathers and a tiny "Ford" emblem. Always in a unique or unusual place and usually at a meaningful time or situation. The intangible signs include electrical and electronic device "malfunctions" that are temporary and unexplainable. Cell phones, lights and clocks doing strange things. The entire electrical system in my nearly new truck shutting down for a few seconds while driving on the interstate, which never happened again. Karen having a bad day and yelling at Drew for not leaving her any recent signs, only to come out to start her car and find everything turned on; lights, wipers, radio and fan on full blast. How could we be certain that was a sign? Because Drew had done that occasionally when he was using our vehicles.

One particular morning in December of 2015 came some song lyrics that forced me to think something more was meant for me. The lyrics I awakened to were: "Operator, well could you help me place this call" followed by "So I can call just to tell 'em I'm fine, and to show I've overcome the blow." This somehow felt like it meant something more than just a phone call. I had an overwhelming feeling that I was meant to be an "operator" to help spirit "place the call" and relay the message, or "tell 'em I'm fine." Me? The skeptical guy who had never believed in afterlife communication?

Visitation Dreams

In late December of 2013, a co-worker of mine and Drew's told me about a dream he had one night. Despite a big age difference, this co-worker named Paul had bonded with Drew during the few years they had worked together. Drew had gained his respect by being a hard worker and their similar brand of humor made for a comfortable friendship. Paul's told me that his dream was vivid and lifelike. In the dream, Drew was walking slowly from right to left at the opposite end of the warehouse. Paul called out to him several times in the dream but received no answer.

Then a few days later another co-worker confided in me a visit she had. Pam is a little older than me and she bonded with Drew from the first time they met. Drew had a couple pet names for her and we all called her his "second mom." Drew had confided in her his relationship with his girlfriend Kes, that he wasn't comfortable telling us about. Pam's vison was not a dream but a waking visit from spirit. She was lying on her bed, on her back with her eyes closed and a blanket covering her. She felt the blanket tighten against her body as if someone were above her, pushing on the sides of that blanket. When she opened her eyes, expecting to see her husband, Drew was there. He didn't say anything to her but she felt his calming presence. She was not as startled as you might expect and informed me that she had seen visions before, when each of her grandparents had passed.

The following week, after being told of the visits by Paul and Pam, I had my first visitation dream. I was awakened at exactly 4:15 a.m. with the most incredible sense of peace, calm and love imaginable. I wrote down the details of this dream right after I woke up. The dream started with Drew and myself walking along a street, somewhere in the northwest part of town. I felt that we were looking for a place with enough room for him to throw his shot put, which he was carrying up on his shoulder. The next thing I remembered, we were somewhere else on an outdoor patio. This place seemed like a restaurant, maybe one with an outdoor beer garden area. I walked outside from a large door, as I donned a hooded rain jacket. Drew was standing at a foosball table, also wearing a hooded rain jacket. He was waiting to finish a foosball game we had started. The score was tied 9-9 and he really wanted to finish this game, despite the fact that it had just started raining. That was the end of the dream. No words were spoken per se. Just as when I do psychic medium readings now, the "words" I received were somehow "felt" by me and I just "knew" what the conversation was. This dream was what is called a visitation dream.

Like most dreams people have, the situations were symbolic. I did not know that at the time of the dream but have since learned much about dream interpretation. The street, destination and shot put, were symbolic of a destination and event that no longer matter. Mundane life events have been left behind and he has now made the journey home to another existence. The foosball game was also symbolic. Drew and I had never played foosball together. We played pool, bubble hockey and air hockey many times but never foosball. This game was symbolic of my spiritual connection with him and my spiritual journey. The tied score represented my situation. I was "on the fence" about my spiritual awakening and it could go either way. He was insistent on finishing the game, which was symbolic of pushing me to make the decision about awakening. The impending rain symbolized the importance of making my decision now. The weather would be much worse, meaning my emotional life would be much worse, if I did not make the decision to awaken spiritually.

Coming Clean

I had seen and heard enough. After experiencing all the signs, ringing ears and a lot of internet research it was becoming clear that I was experiencing a spiritual awakening and there really might be something on the other side, after life. I started looking into local mediums on the internet. Feeling a sense of urgency, I opted for someone who was available at an earlier date than the others. I got up from my desk, walked out to the living room and asked Karen "what would you think if I wanted to see a medium." The look on her face was memorable and priceless. Shock, disbelief, relief and a little joy, all wrapped up in one expression. Remember, I was the one who made fun of her for watching TV shows about mediums. She wholeheartedly agreed and I filled her in with a summary of the research I had done and what I had discovered. In effect, "coming clean" about my evolving beliefs. As it turned out, she was secretly setting aside money to see a medium on her own because of my skepticism. So I returned to my desk and sent an email to the medium, requesting an appointment. It was December 12th and I had a week long business trip to Las Vegas scheduled in about a month. Karen would be accompanying me on this trip and we wanted to have a reading before leaving town. Our appointment for a reading with Kevin was set for the first week in January.

Kevin came to our house for the appointment and we had no idea what to expect. Eric knew who we had coming over that evening and arranged to be away from home. He was not in a place spiritually to accept these beliefs and we respected his wishes. The first spirits to come through for Kevin were who we believed to be Karen's grandmother and aunt. A couple spirits who may have been two of my uncles also showed themselves to Kevin. He was not able to connect with Drew. A young, light haired woman kept being shown to Kevin and we were able to narrow it down to Drew's last girlfriend, Kes. Drew wanted her to be present before coming through in a reading. I thought this was a little unusual but we agreed to schedule another reading. We hadn't met Kes prior to Drew's passing and didn't know her very well. However, during his time in the hospital, she spent more time in his room at his side than most of our family members. The discussion turned to signs, awakening and abilities. After hearing of everything I had going on spiritually, he thought I was awakening and had potential to connect on my own. The skeptic in me wanted to say that was ridiculous but the grieving father in me was willing to try anything. Kevin didn't want to accept payment for that reading because it was less than stellar but I insisted on paying him for his time.

Our second reading with Kevin was just a few days later. Karen, Kes and I sat down with Kevin at his home. Drew came through with some validation and vague messages. The most memorable takeaway from this reading was something Kevin was shown about our upcoming trip. He saw three things that we were to see on our upcoming trip. The first was some kind of multiple lined gold border. The second was a large number "2" and the third was a black and white snake. He explained that the snake was not real or anything to be afraid of but looked more like a drawing of a snake. We flew into Los Angeles to visit my sister and then drove to Las Vegas for the business portion of our trip. Most of our spare time was spent walking the strip, visiting every casino and looking for anything resembling the three things we were supposed to see. We didn't see anything close in resemblance anywhere and were discouraged that we hadn't seen our validation signs. On Friday morning we drove back to the Los Angeles area to visit a client. When we arrived at the client's property, he was outside and greeted us. We talked as he showed me the facility. In my immediate view was a vehicle with decals of alternating gold and black stripes. The black blended in giving the appearance of gold stripes. As we walked just to our right, there was a large rock about three feet high with a flat front surface. On that surface was an engraved number "2" painted red. My client then pointed out another rock nearby that was a little smaller. On this rock was painted a black and white snake with a warning to beware of rattlesnakes. Once we got in the car to leave, I asked Karen if she has noticed the three signs and we agreed this was what we were meant to see.

The Greatest Sign

When we returned home from that Las Vegas and California trip, we discovered the greatest sign from Drew to date. There is a little background behind this story. One evening, prior to the trip, Karen was downstairs in Drew's man-cave and felt a sudden urge to take photos of everything in his room. She photographed absolutely everything from multiple angles without knowing why. Two months had passed since that fateful morning and Eric still would not go down to the basement. We had to do his laundry and he would not enter the house through the garage, which adjoined the basement.

We returned from the trip on a Sunday evening. It was our first trip away from home since the day Drew left us. We missed Eric and we missed Drew. Eric got a hug and Karen went downstairs to Drew's man cave. I heard her loudly and sharply say "Steve, come down here." There wasn't as much urgency for me as there would have been in the past. I had just seen Eric and he was fine. Nothing in that basement could possibly be worse than what had already happened. So I walked down the stairs to find Karen standing in front of Drew's Christmas tree. He had his own tree. It was artificial, about two feet tall and fluorescent green. It held his pink striped tie and two flat penguin ornaments. Karen asked if I had done anything with his tree. No, I had not. She pointed to the ornaments, which were facing away from us and informed me that they had been facing forward before we left for the trip. After showing me the photo she had taken with her phone before we left, she went upstairs and asked Eric if he had been in the basement. His reply was an animated "no" preceded by an expletive.

We began examining the photos side-by-side and even sent them to my iPad for closer scrutiny. Nothing else in the photos had changed. Only the two ornaments that were now facing the opposite direction. Nobody else was in the house and we knew Eric wouldn't, couldn't have done it. This was a sign. An amazing and wonderful sign from our son. The greatest sign!

Drew has since moved the ornaments two more times and it seems to be when we stop paying attention to the tree. That tree is now our only Christmas tree and sits in front of our living room windows, on the sofa table he built in high school shop class.

My First Reading

Kevin had been serious about helping develop my abilities and invited us to a small intuitive development group. We went around and introduced ourselves, then began a general discussion of intuitive abilities. The conversation turned to signs Karen and I were receiving and my awakening symptoms. Everyone there had experienced most of these things, which put us at ease. After about 30 minutes of discussion, we were paired up to attempt readings. My partner for this exercise was Crystal and Kevin started with us because I was totally new to this but he expected me to be successful.

With some instruction and encouragement from Kevin, I was quickly able to visualize three spirits in my mind's eye. The two most prominent I described as "Ma & Pa Kettle." I then asked the most prominent spirit to come forward and it was the male. I felt a fatherly energy from him and related that to Crystal. I asked him to show me a meaningful object and he presented an old-fashioned whistling tea kettle. All of this took much longer than the few seconds it takes to read it here. When I opened my eyes and looked at Crystal, she had somewhat of a stunned look on her face and appeared to be a little emotional.

Kevin asked her to relate anything meaningful she could about what I had described. Crystal was also somewhat intuitive and believed the man I saw was her uncle. I felt the fatherly energy from him because this uncle was like a father to her. The tea kettle related to her experience as a small child. Her uncle would boil water in an old-fashioned tea kettle and she stood in front of the stove waiting for the kettle to whistle. That was a frequent and memorable experience she shared with her uncle. Another subtle validation was the phrase "Ma & Pa Kettle" with "kettle" being the operative word. I was not aware at the time that spirit often show images to elicit a response in the form of a key, recognizable word or phrase. All in all, this brief exercise was a success and left me wondering if I could be a medium.

I was hooked. We began attending Kevin's weekly group on a regular basis over the next several months and I got a lot of practice with many different people. My validations were usually meaningful and recognizable, consisting mostly of clairvoyant visions. Clairaudience, or "hearing" with the inner ear was the next gift to develop for me. Then came clairsentience and claircognizance, or "feeling" and "knowing." During this time of my development, I was also doing frequent readings for Karen.

This was convenient as I had not met most of her extended family, so we were confident I wasn't confusing anything I already knew with what I was receiving from spirit. Every reading involved clairvoyant visions and information from at least one other "clair" sense. In addition to "seeing" I was now "hearing" words and phrases from spirit, "feeling" illnesses or methods of passing and "knowing" the messages spirit wanted to relay through me. Before long, I was a helpful member of Kevin's group, or "class" as it was being called, regularly assisting newer members with growing their gifts. My readings were becoming easier and more than just validation of faces, places and objects. Meaningful messages from spirit were a regular occurrence and I was becoming more comfortable with the process. Karen and others in the group were encouraging me to actually become a medium.

Helping Others

From the very beginning of my development as a psychic medium I felt it was my purpose to help others. My communication with the souls of people's loved ones, especially the soul of my son, had contributed more to the healing of my grief than any support groups we had attended. I had a strong desire to share these gifts with others and help them heal as I was. The people I felt a most urgent need to help were parents who had lost a child and those who had lost someone to suicide. Having experienced both of those types of loss with Drew's passing, I was compelled to reach out and help.

I reached out by setting up a page on the predominant social media site and offered free readings for child loss and suicide survivors. The first inquiry I received was November 1, 2014 which was exactly one year after the passing of my son Drew. I did about fifty free readings over the next month, with a very high success rate for validations. During a medium reading, a validation is something you receive from spirit, validating for your client that you are receiving from their loved ones. There was a particular weekend about halfway through that month when something unusual happened. Because I didn't yet have a business phone, most of the readings at that time were via text message. On four occasions that weekend, my initial clairvoyant visions were not a recognizable spirit of a loved one. What they were in fact, were visions of the client and their surroundings in real time. These were rather detailed, recognizable and unmistakable to the client in every instance. Since these experiences weren't any ability known to me, I researched and eventually discovered it to be called "remote viewing." These episodes of remote viewing do not happen often and I have yet to determine why I receive these visions for any particular client.

While I was able to offer some peace and comfort to others, some unwelcome situations were arising. On a few occasions, I would contact the potential client at our pre-scheduled time and find that they were busy or had forgotten about our appointment. This is somewhat understandable but what bothered me was the fact that their time slot was now wasted. A time slot that could have been taken by someone willing to fulfill their commitment.

Also on November 1, 2014, I was contacted by a woman from Iowa. She was coming through Omaha in a couple weeks with her daughter-in-law and wanted me to do a reading for them. I didn't have an office, so we agreed to meet in the lobby of the hotel they were staying at. We met, chatted a little in the crowded lobby and moved to the pool area for some peace and quiet. I don't typically remember much about the readings because I am not meant to and it would intermingle other people's memories with mine. However, I still recall memorable and profound moments from certain sessions. In this case it was the spirit of a young man named Aaron. His mother and wife were the clients. I was unknowingly feeling my left ring finger with my right thumb and forefinger, while he was showing me a ring and a fire. I kept getting the same two things alternating back and forth. Ring, fire, ring, fire... I opened my eyes to ask if that meant anything to my clients and his wife was visibly moved. She had lost the wedding ring he gave her, in the fireplace. That was one of many memorable moments from readings that has become etched in my memory. I was moved by the expression on her face and the experience was very emotional for me too. Aaron's mother insisted on paying me but I had no rates and had never charged anyone for my services. We agreed on a price and she paid in cash. I still have that $50.00 bill and at some point I intend to frame it along with words of thanks for Aaron.

Testing the Waters

During the course of these several months, I attended some gallery readings by other local mediums and had an individual reading by one. I wanted to see how they all handled their readings and observe their techniques. During a reading with a popular local medium, the conversation turned to my abilities. She asked who I could see for her and an older man came through. He was standing by the back of a pickup truck with a dog. Based on my description, she determined it to be the father of her significant other.

I attended a gallery reading with two other local mediums and afterward, I was compelled to speak with one of the mediums named Angie. After waiting my turn and explaining my situation, she seemed genuinely interested and even offered to help me. We set up a time for me to visit her office and do a reading for her. The details are vague but I believe her grandparents came through. I was very appreciative of her time, interest and assistance. She insisted that I allow her to return the favor and we set up another time for her to do a reading for me.

Angie turned out to be a very upbeat person who gives of herself for others. True to her nature, she had committed to a gallery reading early in the holiday season of 2014. The proceeds were to be donated to a local charity and she invited me to partner with her for the event. I had to think about that one. With a lot of prodding from my wife, Karen, I agreed to do this event. I have always been rather shy and averse to public speaking, so this was way outside my comfort zone. When everyone had arrived, there were about 15 people in attendance. Angie was the perfect mentor for me in this environment. She took the lead, passing along her validations and messages, then deferred to me for anything further. In each instance, I had received something during her interactions. The seminal moment of that evening for me was toward the end. We were finishing up for one client and I received an additional vision. To the best of my recollection, I described it as two boys, standing by a broken side window of a car. I believe one of them still had a rock in his hand. There were a few more details I no longer recall. None of this resonated with the attendee we had just finished with. As I looked around the room, a man on the opposite side of the room raised his hand ever so lightly. He had a sobering look on his face and stated that this was him and his friend when they were little. They had broken a car widow at a junkyard and gathered up the small pieces. They then convinced his younger brother that those pieces of glass were diamonds, as part of an elaborate prank. As I received more details, it became apparent that this man's brother was the spirit we were communicating with. He was moved to tears by the experience, as were most of those in attendance. Most notable was this man though. This man, myself and our wives conversed after the event and he stated that prior to that evening, he was the ultimate skeptic. My thought was, this was me just over a year ago! I was also the ultimate skeptic, with one big difference. I was not open enough to let my wife drag me to a psychic medium gallery event. I had now done a complete 180 degree turn in my spiritual beliefs.

Jumping In

After all of the events that had happened in late 2014, I felt my spirit guides were leading me to be a psychic medium. Not just as a hobby but as a vocation. Self-realization of this spiritual calling was comforting, fulfilling and something I enjoyed doing. The peace and comfort I was able to give others was healing for them. That healing in turn, was healing for me. I now believed that nothing helps us heal like helping others heal. My desire was to help people discover their loved ones and their own spirituality. In this ideal world, I hoped to never have a client want or need a second reading. That hope didn't last very long. Within a month, I had clients contacting me to set up another reading. They had more questions and needed more comfort. I soon discovered that not everyone is ready or willing to awaken spiritually. I guess it is easier for some people to pay someone else for things they are unwilling to do for themselves. Having been the ultimate skeptic and then going through a spiritual awakening myself, I thought anyone could do it.

It was time to start charging for my services and set up a Limited Liability Corporation. Legal fees, dedicated phone, website hosting, scheduling and credit card processing services were all expenses I would incur and it was not a certainty that I would recoup the money spent, but I felt pushed by spirit to do this. During the next few months, I continued doing readings, attending groups and learning all I could about mediumship and spirituality. I was also putting the pieces into place for launching my business. I needed a memorable name and I already knew what it would be.

Several months prior, we were at an intuitive group. Everyone was introducing themselves. One somewhat introverted woman gave a very brief introduction, describing herself as being short and an empath. When my turn came, I introduced myself as a tall medium. Since I am 6'5" tall, the play on words elicited a few chuckles and Kevin, the group facilitator, started calling me "Tall" instead of Steve. "The Tall Medium" was my first choice for a memorable name and that is what I ended up using.

By February, 2015 I was ready to launch. I had a legal LLC, phone number, email address, social media page and website with a scheduling interface. After opening up my evenings and weekends for availability, I was now officially a psychic medium. I told the universe to "bring it on" and waited to see what happened. I spent some money on social media ads to get my name out there and "test the waters" so to speak. It was June of 2014 when my bottom line went in the black for the first time. By October, I was getting rather busy. I had set a low rate with the intent of helping people who couldn't otherwise afford a reading but this was starting to consume a lot of my free time. So I raised my rate and offered discounts in selected online groups, geared toward parents of loss. More than half of my clients were not even using the discount codes and business was still increasing. By year end, I had built up quite a bit of money in this bank account, even after taxes. Testing the waters had proven the water to be pretty warm and accommodating.

I was doing a lot of individual readings. Mostly over the phone, with some via video chat. A large percentage of those reading were for parents of loss, who had been referred by previous clients. But I still had not done a group reading on my own. In November of 2015, that finally changed. A young lady named Jackie from a small town about 45 minutes away booked a group reading at her grandmother's home. Was I nervous? Probably ten times more nervous than before my first gallery reading and I wouldn't have Angie there to back me up. I adopted the mindset that this was what the universe intended for me. If I could get through speaking in front of a church full of strangers at my cousin's funeral in 2002, I would certainly be fine in front of a half dozen strangers. I messaged Angie and asked for any advice she could give me. Her advice was just like her, short and sweet: "Yay! Just relax and have fun! Spirit never lets you down!" That first group reading went very well. Just as in my first gallery reading, spirit came through with something profound and convincing for the biggest skeptic in the group. Her name was Cami. When it was her turn, I believe it was her grandfather who channeled through me. His initial message was; "You are going to have to earn it with her. She isn't going to give you anything!" As it turned out, that was exactly what she was thinking. Cami has since opened up and become a true believer. That group reading earned me a glowing review on my social media page by Jackie. Some of her friends read that review and it led to more group readings, while my individual readings also continued an increase in frequency.

Giving Back

Even though my abilities enabled me to pass along peace and comfort for several people, I felt a push to give back somehow. I had previously joined some support groups on a major social media platform and began spending more of my spare time participating in those conversations. That participation quickly became a balancing act. I was now a professional psychic medium and some group members were uncomfortable, feeling as if I were trying to sell them a service. Of those who were uncomfortable, many seemed obviously unaware that I was also a parent of loss. Some were uncomfortable because of their deeply ingrained religious beliefs. I leaned to accept that not everyone wanted the kind of help I was offering. Many parents in those groups were comforted by the words I passed along from spirit for them but it was not enough to overcome the negativity of others. There had to be a better way of reaching those parents who had lost a child AND were open to spiritual communication. The answer was starting my own group.

In July of 2015 I started a new social media group called Grief – Support – Awakening – Hope. It was opened up to anyone experiencing grief, who was also open to spirit communication and the afterlife. I began screening people who requested to join, in hopes of weeding out any potential religious zealots or professionals seeking to build their client list. I was more cautious about who was invited into the group and laid out specific ground rules for types of posts and comments allowed. That group has been open for more than a year and has steadily grown to more than 350 members.

I had begun writing blog entries on my website in November of 2015. Some of those articles were expanded responses to questions asked in social media groups and some were answers to questions posed by clients. My blog was a creative outlet for my intuitive ability but I still had a desire to start a group for parents of loss ONLY. So at the end of June, I started another social media group called Parents of Loss Only. This group would be open ONLY to parent of loss and every parent who requested to join was asked for a photo of their child, along with birth and angel dates. To avoid issues I had experienced in other groups of similar nature, rules were stated from the beginning prohibiting proselytizing. Posts by parents typically involve grief related questions, photos of signs from our children and links to articles helpful in to parental grief process. At this time, there are well over 100 members in this group.

Within a few days of posting my first blog article, I was contacted by a client named Elizabeth who had read it. She lived near a small town where several high school youths had entered a suicide pact. All but one carried it through to completion and the people in this town were devastated by the loss of so many young lives. This client who contacted me was not related to any of the children who passed but the wanted to know if I was interested in speaking to the parents as a group. My unique situation as a parent of loss and a psychic medium could help others heal. But I had only spoken in front of people once before and that was more than ten years ago. What would I say to these parents? I sat down at my computer with a blank word processing document and the words just started flowing. Within an hour I had a brief speech of 1,800 words that I felt summarized the journey I was on. I let Karen read it and she liked it. So I called Elizabeth and read my speech to her over the phone. She liked it and felt it would have a positive impact on parents of loss. She talked to some of the parents from that small town but I still have not heard of any interest in my speech. I continue fine tuning the speech, with the hopes that an opportunity will arise to present my journey of healing to other parents of loss. The experience I gained from channeling that speech would later give me some of the confidence I needed to begin writing this book. Realistically, many people are a little uneasy about the subject of spirit communication and psychic mediums. I believe a majority of parents who have lost a child are open to the concept but intimidated by religious peer pressure and extreme interpretations of scripture. I feel in the depth of my soul that this is a powerful message and the one way to find true peace and hope after the loss of a child. If it is meant to be and when the time is right, an audience will be made available by the universe to hear this message. I believe in the spiritual credo that whatever is meant to be, will be. Since everything happens for a reason, there will be a reason and people who are in need of hearing my words will hear them. Perhaps it will coincide with the release and introduction of this book.

Channeling and Guidance

A couple months into 2016, I began experiencing more specific feelings and words from spirit during readings. The words flowing through me were sounding more like messaging and guidance for the spiritual life path of my clients. Validations were coming very quickly and early on in the readings, as if to make more time for spiritual guidance. Words, then phrases and finally full paragraphs of significant, meaningful messages were now being "channeled" through me in these sessions. What I soon noticed is that very quickly after a reading, I had very little recall of what I had said. It became necessary to find an app for my smartphone to record the readings. I could then email a download link to my clients for them to go back and listen again. After all, this was often urgent, life changing information from spirit and clients often needed to listen to the reading again in a less emotional frame of mind.

Clients were being led to me by their spirit guides to help them identify and discover their spiritual abilities. Some of these clients knew of their abilities, others were unsure and a few were even in outright denial. A typical reading would consist of validation, followed by spirits of the clients loved ones telling me which abilities my clients possessed. Spirit would then channel through me how those abilities would manifest, as well as their best method of relaxation. Along with identifying the abilities, the client was told through me, how they were meant to use those abilities. In most cases, the abilities align with a career path the client had been drawn to and hopefully, was currently employed in. Finally, the client was told who they were meant to help with their gift. Not coincidentally, those people were often those who were going through similar life challenges to what the clients had experienced and hopefully, overcome. Just as I had been pushed by Drew to recognize my spiritual abilities to help other grieving parents and skeptics, these clients were being led to help others through life circumstances they were intimately familiar with. I truly believe that nothing helps us heal like helping others heal.

Included in those being led to me for guidance from spirit, were several other psychic mediums. Not just local but from all over the country. You see, self-discovery can be difficult. It is often when we attempt to look inside ourselves that we lose sight of the forest through the trees. Who best to help with your self-discovery? Someone you trust. Even better, someone your spirit guides trust. Every one of those mediums received deep spiritual guidance from their spirit guides. When each reading was over, I knew which would heed the advice and which would not. I could generally tell from follow-up messages and social media posts, which ones were resisting their path. The feelings I was given by spirit for these clients were valid, but it was not my place to interfere with their free-will choices. Some people learn their life lessons easily and some learn the hard way.

This new twist my channeling and guidance took, brought with it another group of clients. Those newly awakening souls with nobody to talk with about their spirituality. What was the solution? You probably guessed it. Another group! Actually the solution was TWO groups. One for local people that could gather occasionally for discussion and group exercises, another for the remainder scattered across the country. These groups would need to be private, or as the social media site called it, "secret" groups. Let's face it, a majority of people are at least a little freaked out by what we are discussing. Anything from visions, voices and feelings to premonitions and astral projection. Discussing those abilities makes a lot of people uncomfortable. So I created two secret groups and began inviting in clients and people I have met in the intuitive community. The only prerequisite was that I had to know, from spirit that each group member has intuitive abilities.

The Next Step

Spiritual awakening is a continual evolution and discovery of self. What started off for me as seeing signs and receiving visions, progressed through becoming a psychic medium to helping others discover their true spiritual paths. Perhaps a more fitting term would be this is my current mission, subject to change, development and discovery. Many clients want to know what their final path and purpose is. I don't believe we are meant to know that. As I have learned throughout this process, discovery is the most exciting part of journey. It's like the child whose parents tell them to get in the car for a surprise trip. It could be a trip to the grocery store or it could be an adventure to the most amazing amusement park. Trust me, we didn't make life plans with our soul group for a trip to the grocery store! Nonetheless, our path can be altered or blocked by our own free-will decisions. We can choose the "grocery store" mentality and trudge through our mundane existence day after day, or we can hop on the most exciting roller coaster ride ever. There will be twists and turns either way but I can tell you the twists and turns on a roller coaster are more fun than the grocery store aisle. Even if we choose the grocery store, signs pointing us back to the amusement park will continue to seek our attention. We plan for ourselves many opportunities to awaken and find the destined spiritual path. Most people choose to ignore the signs and dismiss the "gut instinct" leading them back to the spiritual path.

So this is what my current mission entails. All things spiritual, having to do with extrasensory abilities or any type of communication with souls, channeling guidance and being a spiritual mentor. Many people have been sent to me by their spirit guides, as a channel to help discover their paths. I am honored to be a part of that path and provide the guidance those people need.

Everything was going well with my business by mid-2016 but the local readings were not seeing the same growth as electronic readings around the country. Karen had been pushing me for months to start doing readings from our home. We had repurposed Eric's old bedroom with new carpet and paint. It now has a decidedly purple feel to it (more like a lavender) since purple is a highly spiritual color. My reservations about this next step were mostly with religious zealots finding my address and causing any number of problems. Some of those religious troublemakers had popped up on my social media page occasionally and had to be blocked. This new home office would also need comfortable furnishings and the room would have to be dedicated to business use only, for tax purposes. By July, I gave in and took the plunge. I began offering readings in my home office. The address would be sent via email after the appointment was scheduled and paid for. I hoped the pre-payment requirement would keep any undesirable people off my door step. I was surprised at how many people began scheduling readings at my home office. We used our nice, padded dining room chairs for a while and it quickly became apparent that I would have to spend some of the nest egg I had built up on furnishings. This room would need to have a welcoming, relaxing and comforting feel to it. So Karen and I set out to find furnishings and décor for the new room. First on the list were blinds and sheer drapes with a lotus flower image and Karen then named it the "lotus room." A sofa, padded armchair, antique secretaire (drop leaf desk) and accent tables completed the furnishings. We found an antique stained glass window resembling a lotus flower for the main wall and dragonfly pattern glass lampshades rounded out the accents. At the time of this writing, the lotus room was ready for readings or a Reiki session with Karen.

The next step is never truly known and always subject to change, based on our free will decisions. I continue my calling as a psychic medium, helping others in grief through my social media groups, while facilitating awakening and development for others in their awakenings. This time in my life seems like somewhat of a pause for retrospection as I await further instructions. Some of those instructions came in the form of a message from Drew, through my intuitive friend Jen. He had been telling her for about a year that I needed to start writing a book. He was an intermittent thorn in her side and one day in late July of 2016 she passed along a brief but stern message. "Get. Going." Here I am less than a month later with nearly 20,000 words written. This book, this subject just feels like a story that needs to be shared. My optimistic nature wants to believe that other parents of loss can find their way through grief to a place of peace and hope, just as I did. That belief has always been the driving force behind my awakening and mission. I am here to find myself and work toward my life plan in unison with the universe. I take comfort in the belief that my words may help some people and knowing that the universe helps those who help themselves.

Why I Was a Skeptic

My lifetime of societal and cultural surroundings had impressed upon me that seeing is believing. Somehow I had developed a pragmatic approach to life. I now know that pragmatic approach was planned by myself, for myself before my soul came to join with this body. There is a reason for everything. My practical, analytical side helps me weed out the pretenders and make informed decisions in more than one aspect of my life. It contributed to my unique perspective of spirituality. I now have a complete understanding of the analytical skeptic and the ability to communicate with souls beyond the physical realm.

Six years of indoctrination in religious school and 18 years of masses and sermons all tried to persuade me that this one religion was true. Never mind the handful of major religions and 4,000+ total religions practiced across the globe. The religion I was raised in professed to be "the one." What an amazing coincidence that so many people believe the religion they were raised with is "the one." I didn't believe and still do not believe that any religion is "the one." I believe there were some prophetic truths in the Bible and those truths are intermingled with historically documented revisions, deletions and additions. Those modifications all served the agendas of various religious and political leaders over the course of time. The resulting mix of stories contains tens of thousands of contradictions that make it open to literal and philosophical interpretations that can fit any agenda. Pick a social, cultural, religious or spiritual issue and state your position. It's a pretty good bet that a diametrically opposing position can also be found in the Bible. These contradictions are not limited to Christianity, nor is the temptation to use interpretations of holy books for nefarious agendas. The bottom line, I believe is that these religions and holy books are used for the purpose they evolved into. To control people through fear and keep them beholden to the religion they believe can save them from whatever potentially horrible afterlife is taught by that religion. While the bulk of that assessment is pragmatic, there is room for spirituality. I agree with the basic tenets of morality, tolerance, respect and love of life, all lives, embraced by people across many religions.

Just as all of us do, my soul planned opportunities for me to awaken along the way. These are referred to as "exit points" in your pre-life soul plan. The most memorable and absolutely certain exit point for me was an out of body experience (OBE) when I was 18 years old. It was a very hot day in July and I was riding my motorcycle eastbound on "O" street in Lincoln toward Cotner

Boulevard. I was riding at or below the posted speed limit of 45 miles per hour and without a helmet. A stopped driver in the oncoming left turn lane suddenly began turning in front of me. Her statement to police was that she didn't see me. The last thing I consciously remember was reaching for my brakes. Eyewitness accounts told of my bike hitting her car and my body flying over the handlebars. I had broken her windshield with my head, flipped over and landed on the street, heels first and unconscious. I recall somehow seeing vivid images from above the scene of the rescue squad arriving and the bystanders around my unmoving body. It was a busy intersection but everything had come to a standstill, with cars and people everywhere. After what seemed like a very brief period of time, I began hearing voices saying "stay down, stay down, stay down…" The same extreme heat that had influenced my decision to ride without a helmet had made the pavement unbearably hot. I was now somewhat conscious and trying to get up off the hot pavement. Bystanders were holding me down as the rescue squad arrived and I regained full consciousness. Physically, I literally walked away from the hospital emergency room with a concussion and (as discovered a few days later) a fractured heel bone. The attending physician informed me that I was the luckiest man alive and I never rode again without a helmet. Spiritually, I came away with unusual feelings. How could I have possibly seen what I saw from above the scene? Was it my imagination or some kind of hallucination? My conscious and pragmatic mind began reasoning away what I had seen but the experience remained filed away in my memory bank awaiting further explanation... some day. This event could also be called a near death experience (NDE) because I certainly could have physically died from the force of my head hitting a windshield at 45 miles per hour. Whatever term is used to describe it, the experience was powerful and memorable. Thirty years later, I finally figured out what it meant.

The Skeptic and Grief

Nobody I was really close to had ever passed away prior to Drew's passing. Perhaps my upbringing around the funeral home culture had contributed to my being jaded toward the process of death and grief. I had experienced shock and denial after deaths of loved ones but nothing compared to losing my son. I had an unexplainable bond with my maternal grandmother. Maybe it was because she had a caring soul, not just for me but for all of her grandchildren. I was about 30 years old when she passed away. There was a visitation the night before her funeral but I didn't want to go in and view her body. Again, the funeral home culture had influenced me. I wanted to remember her as she was, not after what the morticians had done to her and covered up with a bad makeup job. My mother came outside and talked me into viewing her body. The small town funeral home had not done such a bad job. Even so, something inside my soul knew that she was no longer there. I didn't feel sorrow as much as a relief that her battle with physical ailments was over. My pragmatic mind wasn't ready to let me believe that her soul was still around but those feelings were also filed away for future reference.

A few months after my son passed away and I had begun seeing clairvoyant visions in meditation, I saw my maternal grandmother in one of those visions. She was with Drew. I saw her hand a mourning dove to Drew. He then released it into the air, as if setting it free and sending it to me. My memories of mourning doves were from spending time as a child at my grandmother's house in a small town. It was a quiet, peaceful place and I specifically remember the unusual call of a particular type of bird. One day, I asked my grandmother what that unusual sound was. She replied that it was a mourning dove. I thought she meant "morning" dove and didn't have any notion of how their calming "coo" of a dove could comfort someone in "mourning." When I saw Drew and my grandmother in that vision, I immediately recognized the link between the dove and mourning. We had lived in this house for 22 years and had never seen or heard a mourning dove. Within a few days, we had two mourning doves frequenting our house. They stood on the railing of our deck and quickly built a nest on top of a step ladder that was leaning against the back of our house. I now understood the connection and the significance. My grandmother, along with Drew had sent us those mourning doves to help comfort us in our grief. Soon we discovered there was an egg in the nest and the female dove was keeping it warm. It was a warm early spring until we had a week or two of unusually cold weather. We watched the female dove closely as she sat in her nest 24 hours a day. I had ordered some bird feed made especially for doves and one day I decided to see if I could feed her. I poured some bird seed in a small plastic container and walked toward the nest. She actually let me pour out some food for her, literally inches away from her and the nest. I believe somehow this dove knew on a soul-to-soul level that I would not harm her. Over the course of almost three years since Drew's passing, we have had several mourning doves in and around our yard. There are now two in particular that often sit on the peak of our roof and coo, directly above where our chairs are in the living room. We are thankful for those doves that were sent by the souls of Drew and my grandmother to help us in our mourning. Had you told me when I was a child that is was possible for souls from beyond to do things like sending doves, I would have responded in true skeptic fashion, with a look of derision.

Randy, one of my cousins passed away in 2002 at the age of 42 after a battle with cancer. We were not particularly close but I also felt an unexplainable connection with him. Despite being from completely different backgrounds (farmer and city boy) and him being a year older than me, we connected and I always felt comfortable around him. I never thought of the connection or comfort as anything spiritual. When my parents would send me to spend a week on the farm during the summer, I usually did chores and spent more time with Randy. He was the one who didn't call me a "city slicker" and knew that farmers were not the only people with a strong work ethic. When I heard Randy was sent to a hospital in Omaha, I visited him during my lunch hour. I even bought him a book about beating cancer, written by a famous bicycle racer. But the book and his medical care were too little, too late. He was ready to go home with family and friends, to look at the corn fields in the time he had left. When I heard of his passing, I felt compelled to do something, say something to honor this man in some way. So I wrote something entitled "That was Randy" with the intention of reading it at his funeral service. I had never spoken in public before and had no idea why I wanted to but I emailed Randy's wife Linda and asked for her thoughts. She checked with "Father Steve" at the church and replied that Randy would be honored if I read my tribute at his service. What I had written seemed brief on paper but it was still 448 words and would seem like an eternity reading it in front of all those people. I was nervous for the entire two hour drive to the funeral and expected to be one of many family and friends with something to say at the service. As it turned out, I was the only one. You could hear a pin drop as I walked to the lectern. Waiting for my voice to crack and trying not to shed a tear, I prepared to speak. An amazing and unexpected calm came over me as I spoke. My words flowed more easily than expected and the entire experience was calming to my soul. At the time, I had no idea why it was so easy. I most certainly didn't consider it anything spiritual and pretty much attributed it to the wisdom of my years. I now know Randy was with me in spirit, giving me the strength and comfort necessary to express these words of honor.

My paternal grandmother and two more uncles also passed away in the late 2000's and early 2010's but none of those losses were enough to push me toward a spiritual awakening. To the skeptical me, death was death. Whether or not there was anything else for a soul after life was unproven and not a pressing matter for discussion. Perhaps I was too busy with my mundane life and the losses were not close enough nor deep enough to trigger any philosophical or spiritual introspection.

Why I Awakened

The death of a child is the deepest and most profound emotional pain anyone can experience. I have not yet met anyone who would argue that point. Unless one had experienced the death of a child, I would most likely not entertain their argument on this issue. What other traumatic life event could possibly be a greater catalyst for spiritual reflection and curiosity about the afterlife? When I was faced with losing a child, I was immediately open to absolutely any possibility of communicating with his soul. That openness was a constant gut feeling that overpowered my conscious mind. Every deep-seated belief I had held for my entire life was thrown out the window. Shock, denial, guilt, blame, anger and many other unimaginable emotions were thrust upon me. Those emotions were overwhelming at first but became easier to process as I awakened and began discovering the true nature of life and death.

To my old self, death was death. The end. That belief changed as I experienced all the signs from the soul of my son and he pushed me to awaken. Why? Because it was my plan. I now believe that we all plan for ourselves, opportunities to awaken spiritually and discover the abilities we all have hidden away inside us. Some of us take that opportunity and some don't. I can tell you emphatically that grief is a much different process for those who are open to spirituality and the afterlife. Or, as I refer to it, "between" lives. The term afterlife implies that life is a one-time experience. Nothing could be further from the truth. There are many books explaining the concept of pre-life soul planning and reincarnation, so I won't go into it in depth here. Suffice it to say, our souls come here to human form over and over again. We have a "soul family" that we repeatedly share human experiences with, each time in different relationships.

Religion had no influence in my belief system before my life change and it still does not. Nor did religion, or lack thereof play any part in my spiritual awakening. Although spirituality can lead some to, or away from religion, there is a distinct difference between religion and spirituality. The two are not synonymous as many people believe. I understand why some people have the need to let their spirituality be controlled by religious leaders. Perhaps the best explanation came from a co-worker who said, in effect he was covering himself "just in case." Given his intolerant world view, I can't help but think that if love and light were actually demonstrated in some people's views toward others, religion might have closer ties to spirituality. I find it troubling that so many self-professed Christians choose not to live by the documented teachings of Jesus. But I am not here to judge. Just don't push your interpretations of the Bible on me or anyone else and we can agree to disagree.

This is where religion played an indirect role in my awakening. Answers. The parents of loss I interacted with found no useful answers for grief in the Bible. Not to pick on Christianity specifically but it is the only religion most of us are familiar with. As I discovered more about spirituality, afterlife, spirit communication and the universe the answers became clear. Everything I discovered resonated with me. I began to feel that as if I were re-learning something I already knew on a soul level. Unlike the thousands of contradictions in the Bible, the pieces fit together and made sense. It was easy to have faith when one teaching didn't contradict another teaching. The convoluted mess of contradictions I had been taught to believe was easily replaced by universal truths I trusted with my heart and soul. I am excited to share my beliefs and experiences with anyone who approaches me with a genuine interest. In contrast to some religions, I have found that highly spiritual people generally have no desire to seek out people force their beliefs on. Those who have awakened understand that everyone is following a path.

The universe will help put people and situations in place along that path to steer you toward awakening. When the time and situation are right, "gut instinct" is there to confirm it. Generally, if you have to "force it" then the time isn't right for you. For me, the time was right and all the pieces fell into place to make it happen. If you embrace the universal concept that everything happens for a reason, opportunities are easier to recognize in the present and in hindsight.

A perfect example of all the pieces falling into place for me is Kevin, the first medium we saw, who introduced me to mediumship. He recently moved to a rural area and is no longer a practicing medium. His role in my awakening took place during a time when that window of opportunity was open for it to happen. Not to say that I wouldn't have awakened and found my spiritual calling without him but it may have taken longer and been more difficult. There have been many others who have contributed in some way to my spiritual awakening. Some are still part of my journey and some are not. Not everyone is meant to walk with you for your entire spiritual journey. I am comfortable enough with myself to release those whose intentions do not serve my soul and the greater good of the universe. Many people hold the belief that their current path is taking them in the right direction, even as their spirit guides are trying to push them in a different direction. As I always say; "Beliefs are individual. Truth is universal." Just because you believe something does not make it a universal truth and universal truths do not change just because you don't believe them. Spiritual awakening is called that because our spirit is truly "waking up" to the truths of the universe. Upon awakening, we begin to discover more of those truths. Some people can't handle the truth and resist further awakening, clinging to beliefs rooted in darkness and fear. I chose to release those beliefs and move toward light and love. That light and love in turn leads me to peace, comfort, patience, tolerance, understanding, compassion and a sense of oneness with the universe. And that is why I awakened.

The Big "Why?"

This was the most important question since those first days in the hospital with Drew. Why did he do it? The answer I was looking for took me down an emotional and mundane path. There are no true answers along that path. The only answers I found that were comforting and made sense were spiritual in nature. As Karen and I became more involved in the spiritual community, we attended groups and met other mediums. Remarkably, three of those people we met on different occasions each related similar accounts. These three people didn't know each other and we were confident in their abilities to communicate spiritually. The common factor in each account had to do with Drew's pre-life soul plan. He had planned, with his soul group, his maximum lifetime point. That point was his 21st birthday, which was three weeks away at his time of passing. We were also told by these three people of a horrific automobile accident that would have happened before his 21st birthday. That accident would have left Drew in a paralyzed and vegetative state, draining us emotionally and financially. We would have had to make the decision to disconnect him from life support and let him pass.

Those accounts were remarkable in their similarity and implications. Karen and I had been reading books about soul planning and this account of Drew's soul plan made sense. Most importantly, it resonated with both of our souls and just felt "right." We began piecing together his life to find the "exit points" he had planned for himself during his life. Exit points are points during our life, at which we connect with our higher selves, decide if we will continue our current physical life and what changes may need to be made to our life or soul plan. There were a few exit points, most notably a fall on the icy steps of my parent's house, when our boys were spending a weekend with them.

The old skeptic in me still drove me to do a lot of research on the subjects of spirit communication and soul planning. That research, combined with what I receive from my spirit guides has given me the ability to inform and comfort other parents of loss. This all felt like part of my own soul plan and something I was drawn to do. Drew is my primary spirit guide for spiritual abilities and he is leading me along my path. This path is how I can best help others who are experiencing loss similar to mine.

It is a big step for most parents to believe that their child was ready to pass on, at a soul level. It is even harder to believe that we planned the entire scenario with them, before incarnating. The spiritual explanation is the only answer I found that made sense and resonated with my soul. There is peace, comfort and hope in knowing that the soul of my son is with me every day, guiding me on my life journey. I could have spent the rest of my life, asking "why" every minute of every day and found no reasonable answers from medicine or religion. I know many parents who are stuck on that path. For them, every day is like day one of their child's passing. I feel for them and offer them my assistance. Whether or not they choose to accept is their individual free-will decision.

If you are a parent of loss or grieving the passing of a close loved one, and you are open to discovering your own spiritual connection to souls of those who have passed, please watch for my next book. It is in progress as the final edits are made on this book. The working title is *Awakening from Grief: Discovering Hope in Your Own Spirituality.*

Final Thoughts

I have learned a lot of things on my journey through grief and awakening. Here are a few of them.

- No matter what your life circumstances are, there is someone else who is worse off than you are.

- Nothing helps you heal emotionally like helping others heal.

- Some people are content to be "stuck" in their grief process and there is nothing you can do about it.

- There is nothing you could have done to change the outcome.

- Forgiveness of yourself is as important as forgiveness of others.

- Your circle of family and friends will change after the loss of a child. Embrace those who stay.

- Stay grounded. Physically, emotionally and spiritually. Nature is the best way to stay grounded.
- Seek out avenues to share your grief with others who have similar spiritual beliefs.

Grief can feel like a roller coaster without the safety harness. Awakening is the sigh of relief when the roller coaster stops.

Grief is a process of understanding. If you are not finding the answers, try looking somewhere else.

Your spirituality will determine whether your grief controls you or you control your grief.

Grief is an earthly human emotion we experience because our mind doesn't remember what our soul already knows.

Grieving the loss of my child

Take it one day at a time and don't set any expectations for yourself. Tears of sorrow are healing, so let them flow. It may get better. It may get worse. Accept that whatever emotions come are meant for you. There is no other emotional pain we can experience here on earth as deep as this. You are experiencing the deepest pain and you can emerge as the strongest of souls. We are given the challenges that will make us the strongest when we overcome them. It may not seem like it now but some day you will understand. Accept your feelings. Trust your gut instinct. Follow the path you know to be true in your heart. The journey will be amazing and the destination will be beautiful.

Grief simplified

Mourn the body. Celebrate the life. Embrace the soul.

Hole in Your Heart

Many believe the loss of a child leaves a hole in your heart.

That feeling is the distance between what your soul knows and what your mind thinks.

You have a choice to either look at that distance as an empty darkness, or walk toward it and embrace everything you discover along the way.

Let the soul of your child take your hand and guide you from your darkness.

Learn along the way what the universe has in store for your remaining time.

Think of it as a spiritual reunion of two souls who have shared many lives.

Remember that even though one must exit first, neither ever really leaves.

CPSIA information can be obtained
at www.ICGtesting.com
Printed in the USA
LVHW050425291121
704718LV00027B/1584